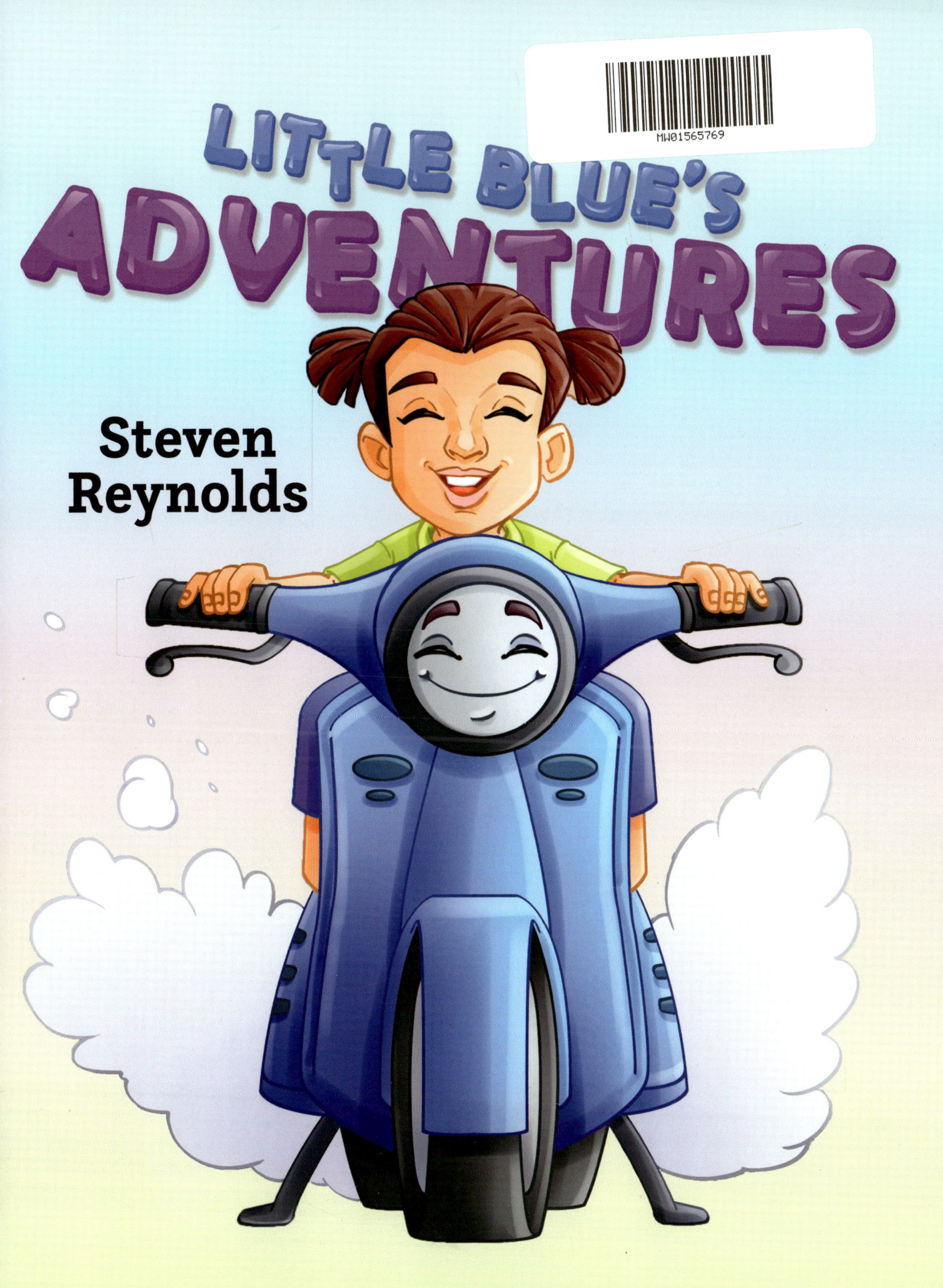

This book was inspired by the blue scooter that took my wife and me on many adventures around Chicago. This book is dedicated to my son and all future explorers.

Little Blue's Adventures
© Steven Reynolds

All rights reserved. This book or any portion thereof may not be reproduced or used in any manner whatsoever without the express written permission of the publisher except for the use of brief quotations in a book review.

ISBN 978-1-66787-481-4

Long ago, when adventures were plenty, there lived a boy who loved riding his scooter, Little Blue.

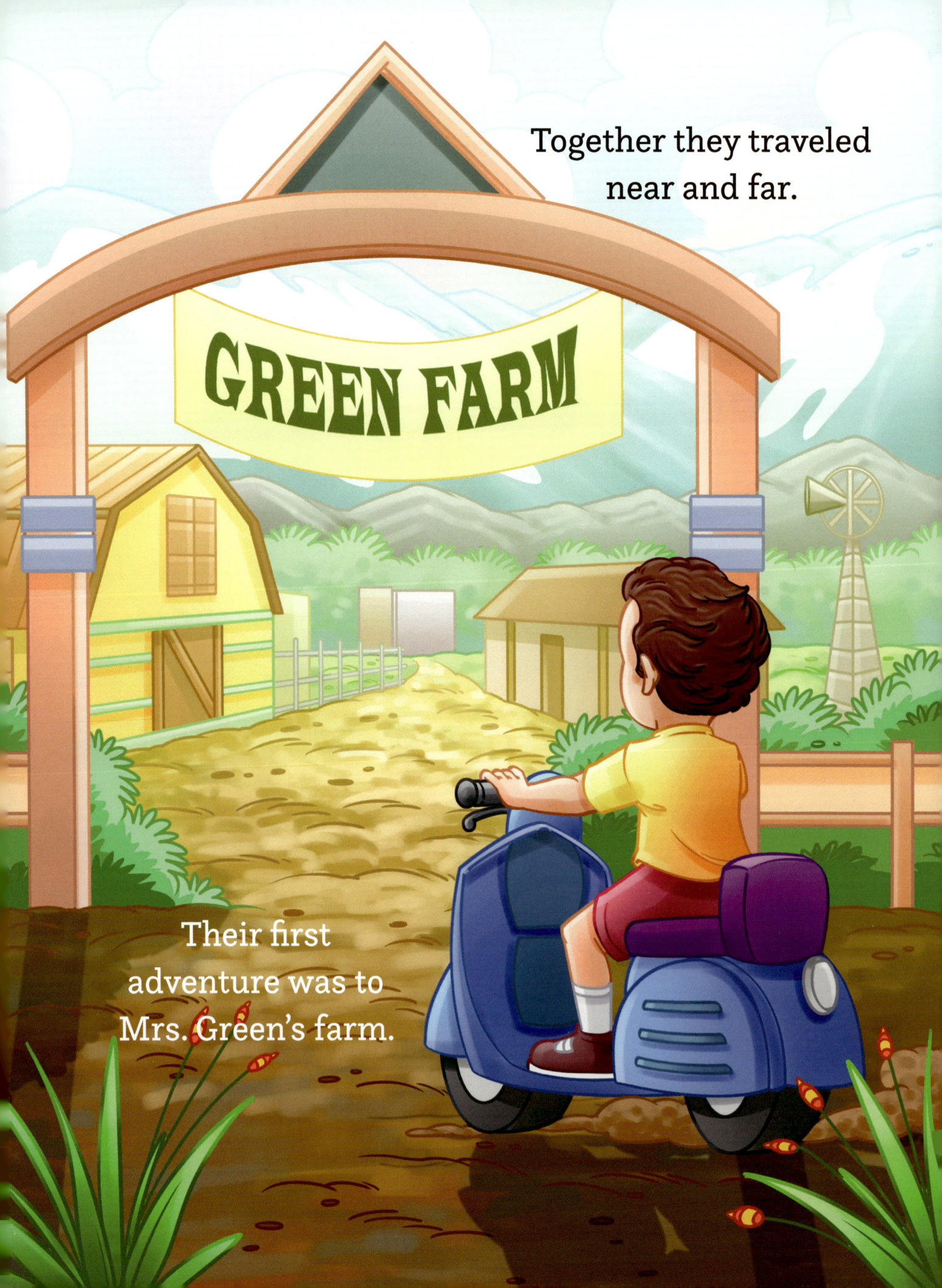

Together they traveled near and far.

Their first adventure was to Mrs. Green's farm.

When they arrived at the farm, Little Blue "beeped" as the boy jumped off to run through the dandelion meadows.

Then they listened to the chickens "cluck" and the cows "moo" while the summer breeze blew.

Their next adventure was along the coast. Little Blue raced the sailboats out to sea while the boy enjoyed the late summer sun.

During the ride, Blue came to a stop with a flat tire.

The little boy worked to fix his scooter. With a little elbow grease, Little Blue was like new!

Time has passed, and the boy is now grown – Little Blue fears he will no longer be owned.

Little Blue doesn't know that the boy is now a Father with a little girl of his own. He loves to share bedtime stories of his scooter adventures with his daughter.

One day, the little girl was playing in her yard when her ball rolled under the shed door.

Her curiosity grew as she opened the door.
What treasures are hidden here?

She was greeted with a big smile and two bright eyes; this was Little Blue, the scooter her Father loved! She asked her dad to teach her all about the scooter.

They rode to the beach since
Blue needed some sun!

The little girl filled her bag with fruits and vegetables, and they set off for home.

On their way home, Little Blue hit some rocks, and she heard a "pop."

She remembered her Father's stories and fixed the tire to get home.

That night, the little girl and her Father both dreamed of their past scooter adventures and those to come.